STECK-VAUGHN

WINNERS

HALLS OF FAME

Melissa Stone Billings

Henry Billings

STECK-VAUGHN
C O M P A N Y
ELEMENTARY • SECONDARY • ADULT • LIBRARY

Books in this series:

Congressional Medal of Honor
Halls of Fame
Olympic Games
Nobel Prize

Acknowledgments

Photo Editor

Margie Foster

Production and Design

Howard Adkins Communications

Cover Illustration

Linda Adkins Design

Photo Credits

P.2 National Baseball Library, Cooperstown, NY; p.3 AP/Wide World; p.4 National Baseball Library, Cooperstown, NY; p.7 AP/Wide World; p.10 National Baseball Library, Cooperstown, NY; p.11 AP/Wide World; p.13 UPI/Bettmann; p.16 UPI/Bettmann; p.17 UPI/Bettmann; p.19 UPI/Bettmann; p.22 UPI/Bettmann; p.23 AP/Wide World; p.24 © Focus On Sports; p.27 AP/Wide World; p.30 © Sheedy & Long/Sports Illustrated; p.31 AP/Wide World; p.33 © James Drake/Sports Illustrated; p.35 © Focus On Sports; p.38 AP/Wide World; p.39 AP/Wide World; p.41 © Focus On Sports; p.42 © Focus On Sports; p.46 © Sheedy & Long/Sports Illustrated; p. 47 AP/Wide World; p.49 © Sheedy & Long/Sports Illustrated; p.52 © Focus On Sports; p.53 AP/Wide World; p.54 © Focus On Sports; p.58 © Focus On Sports; p.59 AP/Wide World; p.60 AP/Wide World; p.63 UPI/Bettmann; p.66 UPI/Bettmann; p.67 © Focus On Sports; p.68 © Focus On Sports; p.71 © Focus On Sports; p.74 © Heinz Kluetmeier/Sports Illustrated; p.75 © Focus on Sports; p.76 © Focus On Sports; p.80 © Focus On Sports; p.81 © Mickey Palmer/Focus On Sports; p.83 © Heinz Kluetmeier/Sports Illustrated.

The Halls of Fame

Most major professional sports have their own Hall of Fame. These places are really museums. They collect things that have a special meaning in the history of the sport. They also honor players who have been truly great. These players are elected by the nation's sportswriters.

The National Baseball Hall of Fame is in Cooperstown, New York. Opened in 1939, it is the oldest Hall of Fame. The National Professional Football Hall of Fame was founded in 1963. It is in Canton, Ohio. The Naismith Memorial Basketball Hall of Fame was opened in 1968. It is in Springfield, Massachusetts.

Contents

BASEBALL HALL OF FAME

Lou Gehrig

The Iron Horse

On May 2, 1939, Lou Gehrig went to Joe McCarthy, manager of the New York Yankees. "Joe," said Gehrig, "I'm taking myself out of the game today."

"Are you sure, Lou?" McCarthy asked.

"I'm sure," answered Gehrig softly. "I'm not doing the team any good. I don't know what's wrong with me. But I think I should take some time off."

Baseball fans across the country were shocked by Gehrig's decision. "It's not possible!" they cried. "Lou Gehrig always plays. He hasn't missed a game in fourteen years!"

How It All Began

On June 2, 1925, the Yankees played the Washington Senators. Yankee first baseman Wally

Pipp had a terrible headache. He had been having them for weeks. The manager thought it was a good time to give him a rest. "Take a seat today, Wally," he said. "Young Gehrig will play in your spot." Gehrig got three hits and scored a run.

Gehrig's first hit of the season, 1938

Gehrig started the next day and the day after that and the day after that. As things turned out, Wally Pipp never started another game for the Yankees. In fact, no one but Lou Gehrig started at first base for the Yankees until that May afternoon fourteen years later. Over those fourteen years Gehrig played 2,130 games in a row.

Gehrig set many baseball records. He still holds the major league record for the most home runs with the bases loaded—23. He also holds the American League record for driving in 184 runs in one season. He shares the major league record for hitting four home runs in one game.

But the record that stands out above all others is the one for playing in 2,130 games in a row. He played with all sorts of **injuries**. He played with colds and headaches. He played with spike wounds and fevers. In short, he played when other men would have taken a day or a week off. His toughness earned him the nickname "Iron Horse."

injuries
damage done to the body

Gehrig receives congratulations after scoring.

The End of the Line

The first sign that Gehrig was losing something came in 1938. The Yankees won the World Series that year. But Gehrig hit only .295 for the season. It was the first year he hit under .300 since 1925. Gehrig began the season very well, but played poorly near the end. What had happened to his great power?

"I tired in the middle of the season," Gehrig said at the end of 1938. "I don't know why. But anyone can have a bad year. Don't worry, I'll be back next year."

In the spring of 1939, Gehrig worked very hard to get into shape. During spring training, however, his hitting troubles continued. He wasn't **fielding** or running well, either. Sportswriters began to ask if Gehrig's career was over.

Still, when the season opened, Gehrig was the starting first baseman. The Yankees often won, but Gehrig was no help. After eight games, he was hitting only .143. That was nearly 200 points below his **career average** of .340.

His fielding was even worse. Gehrig was so slow covering first base that his teammates had to wait before they could throw the ball to him.

Farewell

So on May 2, 1939, Lou Gehrig took himself out of the game. For the first time in 2,130 games a different Yankee player started at first base. Lou Gehrig stayed with the team, but he never played another game. At the age of 35, his career was over.

fielding
catching or picking up a baseball that has been hit

career
the job that a person does over the course of his or her life

average
the number of hits for every thousand times at bat

In June, Gehrig went to the hospital to find out why he had lost so much strength. There he got the bad news. He wasn't just tired and getting older. He was dying. Gehrig had a very rare **disease**, now often called "Lou Gehrig Disease." It attacked his muscles, taking away their strength. Nothing could be done to stop it. Doctors told Gehrig the disease would soon kill him.

Within a few weeks, baseball fans everywhere had heard the **tragic** news. On July 4, over 60,000 people packed Yankee **Stadium**. They came to see two games. But more importantly, they came to be part of "Lou Gehrig Day." After the first game, a **ceremony** was held at home plate in Gehrig's honor. The 1939 Yankees were there. So were the Yankees from Gehrig's famous 1927 team. Lou Gehrig was honored in several glowing speeches. A shy man, Gehrig kept his head bowed through it all.

At last it was his turn to speak. He paused for a few moments to collect his thoughts. Then he spoke perhaps the most famous words in the history of sports. "You've been reading about my tough breaks for weeks now. But today I think I'm the luckiest man alive. I feel more than ever that I have much to live for."

At that, the great Babe Ruth walked over and threw his arms around Gehrig. Everyone was in tears. It was a moment no one would ever forget. The world was saying good-bye to a great baseball player and a great man.

Soon afterwards, Lou Gehrig was named to baseball's Hall of Fame. The Yankees **retired** the number "4" on Gehrig's uniform. That number

Gehrig rejoins Yankees after learning that he is ill.

would never be worn by any other Yankee. The Yankees also built a **monument** in Gehrig's honor. Less than two years later, on June 2, 1941, Lou Gehrig, the Iron Horse of Baseball died.

monument
an object built to honor someone

Vocabulary Skill Builder

■ Use the clues to complete the puzzle. Choose from the words in the box.

injuries
fielding
career
average
disease
tragic
stadium
ceremony
retired
monument

Across

2. very sad
4. number of hits for every thousand times at bat
7. set aside
9. damage done to the body
10. an object built to honor someone

Down

1. going after a ball that has been hit
3. the work done over the course of a life
5. special act that is part of an important event
6. place where baseball is played
8. sickness

Read and Remember

■ Answer the questions.

1. How did Lou Gehrig earn the name "The Iron Horse of Baseball?"

   _____

2. What was the first sign that something was wrong with Gehrig?

   _____

3. What did doctors tell Lou Gehrig in June of 1939? _____

   _____

4. What did Babe Ruth do after Gehrig spoke at "Lou Gehrig Day?"

   _____

5. How did the Yankees honor Lou Gehrig? _____

   _____

Write Your Ideas

■ Pretend you are Lou Gehrig. Write a letter to a friend explaining why you feel like "the luckiest man alive."

Dear _____ ,

_____

_____

_____

_____

_____

_____

_____

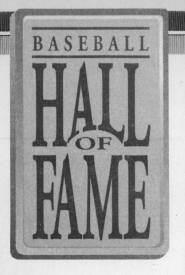

Roy Campanella

The Pride of Brooklyn

Roy "Campy" Campanella met his friend Jackie for dinner in October, 1945. "You know, Campy," said Jackie, "I'm going to be playing ball with the Dodgers soon."

Campy nodded. He had heard a new Negro League team was forming. "So you'll be a Brown Dodger," he said.

"No," said Jackie. "I'll be a Brooklyn Dodger."

stunned
amazed

Campy was **stunned**. But he was also thrilled. At last an African-American would be playing in the major leagues!

Breaking the Color Barrier

contract
work agreement

Campy's friend was Jackie Robinson. A few days later, Robinson became the first African-American to sign a **contract** with a major league team. He

10

was signed by Branch Rickey, owner of the Brooklyn Dodgers. It was a bold move for both Rickey and Robinson. In the past, African-Americans had been kept out of the major leagues. Together, Rickey and Robinson broke this "color **barrier**." A few days later, Rickey got ready to do it again. He asked to meet with Roy Campanella.

barrier
something that keeps people or things apart

"Have you signed a contract to play ball next year?" Rickey asked Campanella.

"Not yet," said Campy. He was the star catcher for a Negro league team called the Elite Giants. He hadn't signed his 1946 contract yet, but he figured it was there waiting for him.

Campanella signing contract with president of the Dodgers

"Do me a favor," Rickey said. "Don't sign anything until you talk to me again."

Campy's hopes **soared**. Perhaps he would become the second African-American to play major league ball! Campy could barely believe it. As a child, he had been poor. His mother was black and his father was an Italian **immigrant**. Campy had started playing baseball in the Negro Leagues when he was fifteen. He had been playing for eight years. But he had never dreamed of getting into the majors.

A Man of Courage

Early in 1946, Branch Rickey offered Campy a contract. Campanella thus became the second African-American to break the color barrier. At first he played on Dodger farm teams. Then, in 1948, the Brooklyn Dodgers called him up to the majors. As a 27-year-old **rookie**, Campy showed that he had great power with the bat. He had a strong throwing arm, too.

But being a great player wasn't enough. Campy also had to be a strong person. Some people hated the idea of African-Americans playing in the major leagues. These people tried to make life hard for Campy.

A Sudden End

Campy played ten years with the Dodgers. He helped them win five National League **pennants** and one World Series. Three times he won the **Most Valuable Player** award. In 1957, the Dodgers decided to leave Brooklyn for Los Angeles. The move excited Campy. He hoped the warm California weather would help him play even better.

soared
went very high

immigrant
person who moves to a different country

rookie
person who is playing his or her first year of professional sports

pennants
flags given to the winning team in a league

Most Valuable Player
player who is said to have helped the team the most

These hopes ended on January 28, 1958. As Campy drove down an icy road, he lost control of his car. He later said, "The brakes were useless. I felt a chill when I saw a telephone pole right where I was heading."

Campy's car hit the pole, then flipped over. Campy lived through the accident, but a broken neck **paralyzed** him from the waist down. Although Campy continued to be **involved** in baseball, his playing days were over.

paralyzed
took away all movement and feeling

involved
connected or linked with

Campanella was one of the game's greatest catchers.

13

Vocabulary Skill Builder

Part A

■ Write the best word(s) to complete each sentence. Use each answer once.

Most Valuable Player	**paralyzed**	**pennants**
barrier	**contract**	

In 1946, Roy Campanella was offered a **(1)**_____
to play in the major leagues. That made him the second African-
American ever to break baseball's color **(2)**_____ .
Campanella became a star of the Brooklyn Dodgers. Three times he
was named **(3)**_____ . He helped the Dodgers win five
(4)_____ . Sadly, Campanella's playing days ended when
an accident left him **(5)**_____ .

Part B

■ Match each word with its meaning.

____ 1. immigrant   a. connected with

____ 2. rookie   b. first-year player

____ 3. stunned   c. went very high

____ 4. involved   d. person who moves to a new country

____ 5. soared   e. amazed

14

Read and Remember

■ Some of the statements below are true. Others are false. Place a check in front of the three things that happened in the story.

_____ 1. Branch Rickey refused to let African-Americans play on his team.

_____ 2. Jackie Robinson became the first man to break baseball's color barrier.

_____ 3. Roy Campanella spent eight years playing in the Negro Leagues.

_____ 4. Branch Rickey offered Roy Campanella a contract with the Brooklyn Dodgers.

_____ 5. Roy Campanella told the Dodgers that he would not move to California.

_____ 6. Roy Campanella continued to play baseball even after being badly hurt in a car accident.

Think and Apply—Cause and Effect

■ Complete the following sentences.

1. Roy Campanella had never dreamed of playing in the major leagues because _____

_____

2. Some people tried to make life hard for Campy because _____

_____

3. Campanella was excited about moving to California because _____

_____

4. Campanella stopped playing baseball because _____

_____

Sandy Koufax

The Man With
the Golden Arm

sponsoring
planning

Dozens of students gathered in front of Lafayette High School in Brooklyn, New York. The school was **sponsoring** a trip to Ebbets Field. Anyone who wanted could go see the Dodgers play the Cubs.

"Hey, Sandy," one boy called out. "I didn't expect to see you here. I didn't think you liked baseball."

"I don't," said Sandy Koufax. "I only signed up because it gets me out of school early."

A Change of Plans

Sandy Koufax wasn't kidding. Once in a while he went to see the Dodgers play. But Koufax's real love was basketball. He was star center of Lafayette's basketball team. He was also team captain.

One summer, Koufax joined a neighborhood baseball team. He didn't get many hits and his throwing was wild. But he showed he could throw a baseball harder than any other player. The next year, he played first base for his high school team.

Koufax winding up

In the fall of 1953, Koufax entered the University of Cincinnati. He planned to study **architecture** and play basketball. He made the basketball team right away. The following spring, he decided to try baseball as well. He won a spot as a starting pitcher. In his first two games, Koufax struck out 34 batters.

architecture
the art of designing buildings

Those 34 strikeouts changed everything. Scouts from around the major leagues rushed to see the young pitcher. Six months later, Koufax had agreed to play for the Brooklyn Dodgers.

A Bum or a Hall of Famer?

Koufax reported to the Dodgers' spring training camp in 1955. He was not an instant **success**. Koufax would pitch **brilliantly** in one game, then fall apart in the next. Dodger fans didn't know if Koufax was a **bum** or a **future** Hall of Famer.

Koufax went on like this for several years. He once struck out eighteen batters in one game. This tied a major league record. Still, he wasn't a winning pitcher. His record in 1960 was eight wins and thirteen losses.

Finally, in 1961, Koufax talked to Norm Sherry, a Dodger catcher. "Don't throw every ball as if it had to go through a brick wall," Sherry said. "Throw more curves and slow pitches."

Koufax followed Sherry's **advice**. Almost overnight, he became the best pitcher in baseball. He won the Cy Young Award for best pitcher three times. In 1965, he set a major league record by striking out 382 players. Said a **rival** manager, "Koufax could beat a team of the best hitters who ever lived."

A Bad Arm

In 1966, Sandy Koufax helped the Dodgers win the pennant. But Koufax's "golden arm" was giving him trouble. It was becoming painful for him to throw. Doctors warned that further pitching could **cripple** his arm. And so, at the young age of 30, Koufax

success
person who does well

brilliantly
very well

bum
person who does poorly

future
in the time yet to come

advice
ideas offered to help someone solve a problem

rival
member of another team

cripple
cause lasting harm

quit baseball. In 1972, Sandy Koufax became the youngest player ever **elected** to the Hall of Fame.

elected
chosen by a vote

Koufax releasing pitch

Vocabulary Skill Builder

■ Write a paragraph using these three words from the story.

advice: ideas offered to help someone solve a problem
success: person who does well
brilliantly: to do something very well

_____

_____

_____

_____

_____

■ Read each sentence. Fill in the circle next to the best meaning for the word in dark print. If you need help, use the Glossary.

1. Sandy Koufax planned to study **architecture**.
   ○ a. how to design buildings   ○ b. paintings   ○ c. French history

2. The school was **sponsoring** the trip.
   ○ a. not part of   ○ b. trying to stop   ○ c. planning

3. Some people thought Koufax was a **bum**.
   ○ a. strong hitter   ○ b. child   ○ c. poor player

4. People wondered how Koufax would do in the **future**.
   ○ a. time yet to come   ○ b. time in the past   ○ c. major leagues

5. A **rival** manager said Koufax was one of the best pitchers ever.
   ○ a. famous   ○ b. member of another team   ○ c. long ago

6. Doctors said further pitching would **cripple** Koufax's arm.
   ○ a. make strong   ○ b. damage   ○ c. make people remember

7. He was the youngest player **elected** to the Hall of Fame.
   ○ a. chosen by vote   ○ b. asked to visit   ○ c. allowed to see

Read and Remember

■ Find the best ending for each sentence. Fill in the circle next to it.

1. When he was in high school, Sandy Koufax's favorite sport was
   ○ a. baseball.   ○ b. basketball.   ○ c. football.

2. Koufax was offered the chance to join the Dodgers after
   ○ a. playing for the Mets.   ○ b. two years of high school.
   ○ c. one season as a college pitcher.

3. When Koufax first got to the major leagues, his pitching was
   ○ a. always good.   ○ b. usually bad.
   ○ c. sometimes good and sometimes bad.

4. In 1965, Sandy Koufax set a major league record for the most
   ○ a. strikeouts.   ○ b. games played.   ○ c. stolen bases.

5. Koufax stopped pitching because
   ○ a. he hated baseball.   ○ b. he didn't want to cripple his arm.
   ○ c. he had made all the money he needed.

Write Your Ideas

■ Pretend that you are a sports reporter. You have watched Sandy Koufax pitch during his first year with the Dodgers. Write a short article describing what you think of him.

_____

_____

_____

_____

_____

_____

_____

_____

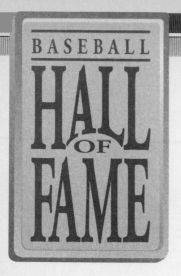

Roberto Clemente

Giving All He Had

Roberto Clemente felt lonely. He had grown up in Puerto Rico speaking Spanish. Now he was playing baseball in Montreal, where most people spoke French. The other players on his team spoke English. Everything and everyone seemed strange.

Clemente was also angry. He couldn't understand what Max Macon, his manager, was doing. As Clemente said, "If I struck out, I stayed in the game. If I played well, Macon took me out. I didn't know what was going on. I was **confused** and almost mad enough to go home."

confused
mixed up

Trying to Hide Clemente

Max Macon wasn't crazy. He was just following orders. The Brooklyn Dodgers had told Macon, the manager of their Montreal farm team, to "hide" Clemente. The Dodgers didn't want other teams to know how good Clemente really was. To keep the secret, Macon played Clemente only when he was having a bad day.

This **scheme** was developed in the spring of 1954. The Dodgers had just signed the nineteen-year-old Clemente for $10,000. That **created** a problem. Under the rules at that time, anyone paid this much money had to play in the major leagues right away. If he didn't, another team could sign him. The Dodgers loved Clemente. But they didn't want him in their line-up right away. So they sent him to Montreal to sharpen his skills with their farm team.

Unfortunately for the Dodgers, the plan didn't work. Clyde Sukeforth, a scout for the Pittsburgh Pirates, saw Clemente play. He told the Pirates, "The Dodgers are trying to hide him. They don't let him play much. But this guy is a **terrific** player. I've watched him warm up before games. He can do everything! And he does it all **extremely** well. My advice? Sign him!"

scheme
plan

created
caused

Unfortunately
unluckily, causing bad luck

terrific
wonderful

extremely
very

Clemente with a small fan

23

A Great Player

On November 22, 1954, the Pirates did sign Roberto Clemente. He played for them for the next eighteen years. During that time he drove pitchers crazy with his hitting skills. Juan Marichal, a pitcher for the San Francisco Giants, said, "The big thing about Clemente is that he can hit any pitch. I don't mean only strikes. He can hit a ball off his **ankles** or off his ear." Pitcher Sandy Koufax was asked if there was a good way to pitch to Clemente. "Sure," Koufax answered, "roll the ball to the plate."

ankles
parts of the body that connect feet to legs

Clemente makes his 3000th hit.

Roberto Clemente won four batting titles and ended his career with a .317 batting average. In 1967, he hit .357, his career high. In 1972, he collected his 3,000th hit. He was only the eleventh player in baseball history to get this many hits.

Clemente ran the bases with great flair. No one went from first to third on a single better than he did. But Clemente was perhaps best known for his fielding. He won eleven straight Golden Glove awards for his play in right field. He had the strongest arm of any outfielder. One manager said, "He can throw people out at second base on balls that would be triples to any other right fielder."

Helping Others

Roberto Clemente was proud to be Hispanic. He felt it was an honor to call Puerto Rico his home. At the end of the 1972 season, he said, "I am proud to be the first player from Puerto Rico to have three thousand hits."

Clemente very much wanted to help his people. He often spoke to groups of Puerto Ricans. He coached a group of young Puerto Rican baseball players. He also worked to build a sports center for the children of Puerto Rico.

Clemente wanted to help people in the rest of Latin America, too. On December 23, 1972, a terrible earthquake rocked the Central American city of Managua, Nicaragua. It killed over 6,000 people and hurt 20,000 more. It left 200,000 people without homes. Clemente was in Puerto Rico when he heard the news. Quickly he went to work to bring **aid** to the people of Managua. He asked Puerto Ricans to give medicine, food, and clothing.

aid
help

Clemente wanted to get these things to Managua as fast as possible. "Some supplies can be sent by ship," he said, "but ships are slow. We need a plane."

Clemente had trouble getting a plane on short notice. At last he rented an old DC-7. He arranged to have it carry supplies to Managua. By New Year's Eve the plane had made two trips. Clemente went to the airport to pack it up for yet another flight.

After the plane was loaded, a friend turned to Clemente. "You've done enough, Roberto," she said. "Take a rest. Go home and spend New Year's Eve with your family."

"I can't," answered Clemente. "There's too much to be done. I'm going to go along on this flight and make sure these supplies get to the people who need them."

At 9:22 P.M. on December 31, 1972, the DC-7 took off from Puerto Rico. On board were Roberto Clemente and four others. As the plane rose into the sky, it turned left over the ocean. Then, suddenly, something went wrong. The plane dropped out of the sky and crashed about one mile out to sea. Everyone on board was killed.

People in both Puerto Rico and the United States were **heartbroken**. Church bells rang out. Radio stations played sad music. The governor of Puerto Rico, said, "Roberto died helping others. Our children lost a hero and a great example. Our people lost one of their **glories**."

Usually a player has to wait five years before he can be elected to the Hall of Fame. But that rule

heartbroken
very sad

glories
people or things that bring honor and pride

was put aside in Roberto Clemente's case. In 1973, just months after his death, Roberto Clemente was elected to the Baseball Hall of Fame.

Clemente visits with his wife and sons at a game.

Vocabulary Skill Builder

Part A

■ Match each word with its meaning.

_____ 1. heartbroken   a. unluckily

_____ 2. ankles   b. mixed up

_____ 3. aid   c. help

_____ 4. created   d. filled with sadness

_____ 5. confused   e. body parts that connect feet to legs

_____ 6. unfortunately   f. caused

Part B

■ Read each sentence. Fill in the circle next to the best meaning for the word in dark print. If you need help, use the Glossary.

1. The Dodgers' **scheme** did not work.
   ○ a. private plane   ○ b. plan   ○ c. list of players

2. Clemente was a **terrific** player.
   ○ a. slow   ○ b. proud   ○ c. wonderful

3. People were **extremely** sad when they heard the news.
   ○ a. not a bit   ○ b. very   ○ c. quietly

4. Puerto Rico had lost one of its **glories**.
   ○ a. reasons to be proud   ○ b. battles   ○ c. ball games

Read and Remember

■ Some of the statements below are true. Others are false. Place a check in front of the three things that Roberto Clemente did.

_____ 1. Roberto Clemente coached a group of young Puerto Rican baseball players.

_____ 2. Clemente became a star player for the Brooklyn Dodgers.

_____ 3. Roberto Clemente tried to hide the fact that he was Hispanic.

_____ 4. Roberto Clemente got 3,000 hits in the major leagues.

_____ 5. Roberto Clemente was in Manaqua, Nicaragua, when a terrible earthquake hit the city.

_____ 6. Roberto Clemente died in a plane crash while trying to get food and medicine to Nicaragua.

Think and Apply—Drawing Conclusions

■ Finish each sentence by writing the best answer.

1. Roberto Clemente felt out of place in Montreal because _____

_____

2. The Pirates signed Clemente because _____

_____

3. Roberto Clemente worked to build a sports center for the children of Puerto Rico because _____

_____

4. Roberto Clemente did not go home on New Year's Eve, 1972, because _____

_____

5. Roberto Clemente rented an old DC-7 instead of a new plane because _____

Bill Russell

The Man Who Changed Basketball

*F*ourteen-year-old Bill Russell slammed his school books on the table.

"What's wrong with you?" asked his older brother Charlie.

"I didn't make the team," Bill muttered. "The coach said I was too thin and **clumsy** to be a good basketball player."

Charlie put his arm around Bill. "Don't worry. That's just because you're tall for your age. You'll make the team next year."

Making the Grade

Bill Russell never did make the basketball team in his Oakland, California, junior high school. He made the high school team, but he didn't play much. In his last year of high school, Russell

clumsy
awkward, not moving smoothly

became a starter. But he was no star. He never scored more than fourteen points in a game.

Most college coaches didn't think much of Russell's record. One person, however, saw something in Russell. Hal DeJulio was a coach

Russell snags ball away from Lakers.

for the University of San Francisco. He saw that Russell could block shots. "I'm telling you, this kid might turn into a great **defensive** player," DeJulio said.

defensive
trying to keep the other team from scoring

So USF offered Russell a chance to play there. The school wasn't much of a basketball power. It didn't even have its own court. Yet it was there that Bill Russell became a great player. His body filled out and he developed strong muscles. He learned to move his tall, 6-foot-9-inch frame with grace. Soon he was playing center like no one had ever played the position before. By his junior year, 1954-55, Bill Russell was the best college player in the country. And the University of San Francisco was the best college team in the country.

Russell later wrote about that year. "We went for all the marbles and it was a crazy, wild sleigh ride that never stopped. We were going hot. Then we ran smack into UCLA (University of California at Los Angeles). They beat us 47 to 40. But that was the last one we lost. From there we just took off, with 55 straight **victories**."

victories
games won

championship
contest held to see
which team is best

The University of San Francisco won the national college **championship** that year. It won again in 1956. During that time, Russell scored an average of twenty points a game. That was good, but not great. What made Russell great was the way he **rebounded** and blocked shots. He once had 62 rebounds in a single game! No one kept records of blocked shots in those days. But if someone had, Russell would have broken all the records.

rebounded
got the ball after a
missed shot

A New Style of Play

In 1956, the Boston Celtics of the National Basketball Association (NBA) picked Bill Russell to play for them. For several years, the Celtics had been a pretty good team. They never won championships, but they often finished second.

Russell has won many awards.

The Celtics could score lots of points. But they didn't have much defense. They couldn't keep the other teams from scoring. Then along came Russell. He gave the team what it had been missing. In his thirteen years with the team, the Celtics won eleven

NBA championships! No **professional** team in any sport has won so many titles in such a short period of time.

Russell did more than help his team win games. He helped change basketball from a slow sport to the fast-paced game it is today. In the past, teams had expected their center to score a lot. Russell, however, was a defensive center. He blocked shots and rebounded missed shots. Then he passed the ball to another player who would fly down the court for a basket. With his quick hands and feet, Russell seemed to control every game.

Celtics' coach Red Auerbach, was once asked about Russell. "Nothing Bill does surprises me any more," Auerbach said. "He's the greatest defensive player I have ever seen in my life, the greatest of all time. I'll go even further than that. He's twice as good as anyone else."

Beyond Basketball

Bill Russell loved basketball. But he knew that it was only a game. He knew that other things, such as the fight for **civil rights**, were more important. Russell never forgot what it was like to grow up poor and African-American in Monroe, Louisiana. In his book, *Go Up for Glory*, Russell wrote that it had been "a little like floating then slowly drowning in a **vast** sea of tar."

As a well-known basketball player, Russell spoke out against unfair **treatment** of African-Americans. He once refused to play a game in Lexington, Kentucky, because the hotel coffee shop would not serve him and other African-American players. Russell also complained loudly about NBA team owners. He believed these owners had secretly put

civil rights
giving all people the same rights

vast
very large

treatment
the way people act toward someone

limits on the number of African-American players in the NBA. The owners became angry when Russell spoke out about it. But Russell didn't care. He knew it was wrong.

Bill Russell did a great deal to help African-Americans in the world of sports. He became the first professional African-American coach when he took over the Celtics in 1966. He also went on to become a general manager and a TV sports **announcer**. In 1975, the great Bill Russell was chosen for basketball's Hall of Fame.

announcer
person who describes games to those watching on TV

Russell blocks a shot.

Vocabulary Skill Builder

■ Complete the following sentences by writing the missing word(s) in each space. Choose from the words in the box. When you are finished, the letters in the boxes will tell you what team Bill Russell played for.

clumsy	civil rights	treatment	professional	championship
vast	victories	announcer	defensive	rebounded

1. In the 1950's, African-Americans faced unfair ＿＿＿＿ .

☐＿ ＿ ＿ ＿ ＿ ＿ ＿ ＿

2. In 1955, USF won a national ＿＿＿＿ .

＿☐＿ ＿ ＿ ＿ ＿ ＿ ＿ ＿ ＿ ＿

3. Russell's greatest skills were ＿＿＿＿ .

＿ ＿ ＿☐＿ ＿ ＿ ＿ ＿

4. Bill Russell helped fight for ＿＿＿＿ .

☐＿ ＿ ＿ ＿ ＿ ＿ ＿ ＿ ＿

5. What made Russell great was the way he ＿＿＿＿ .

＿☐＿ ＿ ＿ ＿ ＿ ＿ ＿

6. At fourteen, Russell was told that he was ＿＿＿＿ .

＿☐＿ ＿ ＿ ＿

7. Russell led his team to many ＿＿＿＿ .

＿ ＿ ＿☐＿ ＿ ＿ ＿

8. College teams are not ＿＿＿＿ . ＿ ＿ ＿ ＿ ＿ ＿ ＿ ＿☐＿ ＿ ＿

9. Russell became a TV ＿＿＿＿ . ＿ ＿ ＿ ＿ ＿ ＿☐＿ ＿

10. Russell's talent was ＿＿＿＿ . ＿ ＿☐＿

Read and Remember

■ Find the best ending for each sentence. Fill in the circle next to it.

1. On his high school basketball team, Russell was
   ○ a. ordered to gain weight.   ○ b. not a star.   ○ c. shy.

2. In college, Russell developed
   ○ a. a sickness.   ○ b. his voice.   ○ c. his playing skills.

3. In the late 1950's and 1960's, the Celtics became
   ○ a. champions.   ○ b. angry with Russell.   ○ c. weaker.

4. Before Russell, most basketball centers were expected to
   ○ a. rebound.   ○ b. block shots.   ○ c. score a lot.

5. Russell helped basketball become a
   ○ a. game of skill.   ○ b. game of chance.   ○ c. fast-paced game.

Write Your Ideas

■ Pretend you are Bill Russell. A reporter has just asked you why you refused to play a game in Lexington, Kentucky. Explain the situation and give your views on civil rights.

_____

_____

_____

_____

_____

_____

_____

_____

_____

Oscar Robertson

The Big "O"

"Where are you going?" eight-year-old Oscar Robertson called as his two older brothers headed down the alley.

"We're going to shoot some baskets," said Bailey Robertson.

"Can I come?" Oscar asked eagerly.

"Okay," snapped Bailey. "Just don't ask to play this time. None of the guys wants to play basketball with a little kid."

"I'll show them," thought Oscar. "I'll get so good, they'll HAVE TO let me play."

The Making of a Star

Oscar Robertson loved the game of basketball. Even as a child, he practiced whenever he could. Robertson grew up in a very poor family in

Indianapolis, Indiana, in the 1940's. His parents didn't even have enough money to buy him a basketball. Instead, Robertson played with a rag tied into a ball and held together with a rubber band. Sometimes he used an old tennis ball. Sometimes he even used a tin can. He shot at a peach basket nailed to the wall in his yard.

One day, when Robertson was eleven years old, his mother came home with a surprise. "The people I cook meals for threw this out," Mazell Robertson said. She held up a basketball. "It's kind of beat up, but at least it's a real basketball."

Robertson rebounds with style.

Robertson was thrilled. He took it with him everywhere. His mother later said, "Oscar was always bouncing it. He'd bring it to the dinner table, and he took it to bed with him. When the sound of the bumping stopped, we knew that Oscar was ready to go to sleep."

All this practice paid off. Robertson's brothers and the other neighborhood kids finally let him play with them. His mother could see how much her youngest son loved the game. She told him to give up his paper route so he would have more time to play. "It wasn't that we didn't need the money," she said. "But basketball had become so important to him. You've got to give a boy a chance to find himself."

By the time Robertson entered Crispus Attucks High School in 1952, he had turned himself into a star. He led his team to the first **undefeated** season in the history of Indiana high school basketball. Twice his team won the state championship. Along the way, Robertson delighted fans. He **dazzled** them with his **dribbling** and shooting skills.

Although basketball was the most important thing in his life, Robertson had many other **talents**. He was a great baseball pitcher and a fine track star. He once set the city record in the high jump. Oscar also was a good student. His grades put him in the top ten **percent** of his class. He was even in the National Honor Society.

Proving Himself Again

College scouts rushed to watch Oscar Robertson play. Robertson didn't disappoint them. In one game during his last year at Crispus Attucks High School, he scored 62 points. Dozens of colleges

undefeated
having no losses

dazzled
amazed

dribbling
bouncing a basketball

talents
skills

percent
out of one hundred

Robertson aims for the basket.

wanted Robertson to play for their team. Eighteen colleges offered him **scholarships**.

Oscar Robertson chose the University of Cincinnati. In his second year there, he averaged

scholarships
money given to a student to help pay for school

35 points a game. That made him the highest-scoring college player in the country. In one game he scored 56 points. People seeing him play for the first time couldn't believe how good he was. In three years he set fourteen college records.

Robertson dribbles past a defender.

Things were not so easy for Robertson off the court. Some people didn't like him because he was an African-American. He wasn't welcome in coffee shops or movie theaters. Even when he was on the court, some fans yelled out **insults**. Robertson was hurt by this. He thought about dropping out of college. But he stuck with it, and finished with his class in 1960.

insults
things that are said that hurt people's feelings

The Best Ever?

Later that year Robertson signed with the Cincinnati Royals of the National Basketball Association (NBA). Robertson played with the Royals for ten years. During that time he led the NBA in all sorts of areas. Robertson, it seemed, could do everything. He could play **offense** and defense. He could pass, shoot, jump, and handle the ball beautifully.

offense
trying to score points for your team

Today people are **impressed** if a player gets a "triple-double." That means getting at least ten points, ten rebounds, and ten **assists** in a single game. In 1962, Robertson averaged a triple-double for the season—30.8 points, 12.5 rebounds, and 11.4 assists.

impressed
believing that someone has done something special

assists
times when a player helps a teammate make a basket

Surprisingly, Robertson never won a championship with the Royals. The team just didn't have enough other good players. In 1970, he was traded to the Milwaukee Bucks. That season he finally won an NBA championship.

Oscar Robertson won a place in the hearts of fans everywhere. They called him "The Big O." In 1979, he made the Hall of Fame. Today many people think that Oscar Robertson was the greatest basketball player of all time. No one has ever done so many things so well.

Vocabulary Skill Builder

■ Match each word with its meaning.

____ 1. percent

____ 2. undefeated

____ 3. assists

____ 4. scholarships

____ 5. dazzled

____ 6. dribbling

____ 7. offense

a. money given to help a student pay for school

b. out of one hundred

c. bouncing a basketball

d. trying to score points for your team

e. times when a player helps a teammate make a basket

f. amazed

g. having no losses

■ Write a paragraph using these three words from the story.

insults: things that are said that hurt people's feelings
talents: skills
impressed: believing that someone has done something special

_____

_____

_____

_____

_____

_____

_____

Read and Remember

■ Answer the questions.

1. How did Oscar Robertson get his first real basketball? _____

_____

2. Why did Oscar's mother tell him to give up his paper route? _____

_____

3. Why did some fans shout insults at Robertson? _____

_____

4. Why didn't Oscar Robertson win any championships with the

Cincinnati Royals? _____

_____

5. Why do many people think Oscar Robertson was the greatest

basketball player of all time? _____

_____

Think and Apply—Fact or Opinion?

■ Write F before each fact. Write O before each opinion.

____ 1. Oscar Robertson was lucky to grow up in Indianapolis.

____ 2. Even as a child, Oscar Robertson loved to play basketball.

____ 3. Oscar Robertson's grades put him in the top ten percent
of his high school class.

____ 4. The University of Cincinnati is the world's best university.

____ 5. Basketball is a more difficult game than baseball.

____ 6. People should never be allowed to insult others.

____ 7. Oscar Robertson thought about dropping out of college.

____ 8. In 1962, Robertson averaged a triple-double.

____ 9. The Cincinnati Royals were smart to trade Robertson.

____ 10. "The Big O" is a good nickname for Oscar Robertson.

Jerry West

Mr. Clutch

"Come on, Jerry! Use the tips of your fingers more when you dribble," David West told his younger brother. "And keep your head up!"

David could see that his eight-year-old brother had a lot of talent. "Someday," said David to Jerry, "I think you're going to be the best basketball player in West Virginia."

High School Hero

Jerry loved having his brother around. He wanted David to stay in Cabin Creek, West Virginia. But in the early 1950's, when Jerry was still a kid, David West went to fight in the Korean War. He was killed in battle. Jerry was crushed. At the same time, he felt more **determined** than ever to become a great basketball player.

determined
having a strong need
to do something

By the time West reached East Bank High School, he was very good. In one of his first games, he broke his foot. That kept him from playing, but it didn't keep him from practicing. Coach Roy Williams said, "He came **hobbling** in every day just to shoot. You couldn't keep him off the court."

hobbling
limping, having trouble walking

West moves down the court.

In 1956, West led the East Bank team to the state championship. Along the way, he set a West Virginia high school record by scoring 926 points in just 27 games. To honor their hero, the town had a special **celebration**.

celebration
special party

Homesick

West was offered scholarships to many colleges. He chose West Virginia University in Morgantown. At first, West was lonely and homesick in Morgantown. Everything was strange. West did not warm up to other students or to his teachers. His grades were poor. More than once he thought about quitting school.

But Jerry West didn't quit. Slowly he **adjusted** to college life. And he kept playing basketball. In his first year he led his team to an undefeated season. In 1959, he took the team to the **final** game of the national championship.

West Virginia lost the game by one point. But Jerry West was named the most valuable player of the **tournament**.

A Great Clutch Shooter

In 1960, West was signed by the Los Angeles Lakers. He spent fourteen years with them. West proved that he could shoot, pass, and defend with the best. Four seasons he averaged over 30 points a game.

West became well-known for his **ability** to make shots when they meant the most. His teammates called him "Mr. Clutch." In the 1970 championship series against the New York Knicks he made one of the greatest **clutch** shots ever. The Knicks had the lead with just three seconds left in the game. West got the ball and threw it at the basket. The ball sailed 63 feet through the air. To everyone's shock it **swished** through the net.

"If it comes down to one shot," West said later, "I like to shoot the ball."

adjusted
got used to

final
last

tournament
contest made up of several games

ability
skill

clutch
coming at an important time

swished
made a soft, brushing sound

West makes plans with Lakers teammate.

As things turned out, the Lakers lost the game in **overtime**. But no one ever forgot the shot "Mr. Clutch" made to tie the game. Jerry West's brother David had been right. Jerry West was a great basketball player.

overtime
time beyond the usual playing time

49

Vocabulary Skill Builder

■ Use the clues to complete the puzzle. Choose from the words in the box.

determined
hobbling
celebration
adjusted
final
tournament
ability
clutch
swished
overtime

Across

3. having trouble walking
6. having a strong need to do something
7. contest
9. beyond the usual playing time
10. at an important point in a game

Down

1. made a soft, brushing sound
2. skill
4. got used to
5. special party
8. last

Read and Remember

■ Find the best ending for each sentence. Fill in the circle next to it.

1. Jerry's brother David believed Jerry would become a great
   ○ a. soldier.　　○ b. basketball player.　　○ c. coach.

2. When he had a broken foot, Jerry West
   ○ a. stayed in bed.　　○ b. still came to practice.
   ○ c. lost interest in basketball.

3. To the people in his home town, Jerry West was
   ○ a. not important.　　○ b. a trouble-maker.　　○ c. a hero.

4. When he first arrived at college, West was
   ○ a. lonely.　　○ b. sick.　　○ c. happy.

5. Jerry West earned the name "Mr. Clutch" in
   ○ a. the Korean War.　　○ b. a basketball game.　　○ c. school.

Write Your Ideas

■ Pretend you are Jerry West. You are returning to Cabin Creek, West Virginia, to talk to school children. Write a short speech giving them advice about how to succeed in life.

Basketball Hall of Fame

Walt Frazier

Defensive Wizard

quarterback
the leader of a
football team

eager
wanting something
very much

Walt Frazier was **quarterback** of his high school football team. He was so good that he dreamed of becoming a quarterback for the NFL (National Football League).

"That won't happen," a friend said. "You're black. The NFL only wants quarterbacks who are white. Even colleges want white quarterbacks."

From Football to Basketball

When Frazier started checking out colleges in 1963, he found that his friend was right. Several colleges offered him football scholarships. But no one seemed **eager** for him to play quarterback.

Frazier decided to give up his dream of playing in the NFL. He turned to another sport he had always enjoyed—basketball. Frazier accepted a basketball scholarship to Southern Illinois University. In 1967, he helped Southern Illinois become the top basketball team among the country's small colleges. That same year his team won the National Invitational Tournament (NIT). Frazier was named the NIT's most valuable player.

Turning Pro

By then, Frazier had caught the attention of many NBA teams. After the NIT, he signed with the New York Knicks. At the time, the Knicks were a **dismal** team.

dismal
terrible

Frazier is fouled as he tries for a basket.

Frazier waits for a pass.

confidence
a person's belief in
himself or herself

Frazier was not a big-name college star like Oscar Robertson or Jerry West. At first he did not have the **confidence** to turn the Knicks around. In his first season, he averaged only nine points a game.

Things changed in 1968 when Red Holzman became coach of the Knicks. Holzman believed that defense was the key to winning. He told his players to block more shots, steal more balls, and put more **pressure** on the other team.

Holzman saw that Frazier was a great defensive player. Frazier could move very quickly. He was the best man for breaking up plays and stealing balls. With Holzman **guiding** him, Frazier became a **constant threat** to the other team. One player said Frazier's hands were "faster than a **lizard's** tongue."

A Great Leader for a Great Team

In 1970, the Knicks had a chance to win their first NBA championship. By then, Frazier was the man who led the Knicks' attack. He could sense which player had the hottest shooting hand. He made sure to get the ball to that person. Frazier also hit a lot of shots himself. One way or the other, every play seemed to include him. As Willis Reed, the team's center, said, "It's Walt's ball. He just lets us play with it once in a while."

The Knicks' offense had finally fallen into place. But their biggest strength was their defense. Frazier hounded **opponents** all over the court. His lightning-quick hands led to many steals and to many easy baskets. He led the New York Knicks to NBA championships in 1970 and 1973. Twice he was named the best defensive player in the league. Seven times he was named to the NBA's All-Defensive first team. No one knows how good he would have been as a quarterback. But as "quarterback" of a basketball team, Walt Frazier was one of the greatest of all time.

pressure
strong force to do something

guiding
teaching or showing

constant
all the time

threat
danger

lizard's
belonging to a small, quick animal

opponents
players on the other team

55

Vocabulary Skill Builder

■ Write the best word to complete each sentence. Use each word once.

eager	confidence	guiding	dismal	quarterback

In high school, Walt Frazier wanted to be a **(1)**_____ .
But no college football teams were **(2)**_____ for him to
play that position. So Frazier turned to basketball. When he joined
the New York Knicks, they were a **(3)**_____ team. At
first, Frazier did not have the **(4)**_____ to lead the
Knicks. With coach Red Holzman **(5)**_____ him,
however, that changed. Frazier became a star player and the
leader of his team.

■ Read each sentence. Fill in the circle next to the best meaning for
the word in dark print. If you need help, use the Glossary.

1. Walt Frazier put **pressure** on the other team.
   ○ a. ink   ○ b. force   ○ c. stickers

2. Frazier was a **constant** worry to the other team.
   ○ a. all the time   ○ b. comfortable   ○ c. familiar

3. Frazier was a defensive **threat**.
   ○ a. special reward   ○ b. mean person   ○ c. danger

4. One player said Frazier's hands were as fast as the tongue of a **lizard**.
   ○ a. magic man   ○ b. small, quick animal   ○ c. old shoe

5. **Opponents** soon learned that Frazier was a great player.
   ○ a. people who cheer   ○ b. other teams   ○ c. coaches

Read and Remember

■ Some of the statements below are true. Others are false. Place a check in front of the three things that Walt Frazier did.

_____ 1. Walt Frazier played football in high school.

_____ 2. Walt Frazier accepted a college baseball scholarship.

_____ 3. Walt Frazier dropped out of college after two months.

_____ 4. Walt Frazier became very good at stealing the ball.

_____ 5. Walt Frazier never passed the ball.

_____ 6. Walt Frazier was named to the NBA's All-Defensive first team seven times.

Think and Apply—Main Ideas

■ Underline the two most important ideas from the story.

1. Walt Frazier became a basketball star by showing how important it is to have a good defense.

2. The college that Walt Frazier attended was a small college.

3. In his first year with the Knicks, Walt Frazier did not have much confidence.

4. Willis Reed was the center of the New York Knicks in the early 1970's.

5. Walt Frazier helped change the Knicks from a dismal team into a championship team.

Gale Sayers

Touchdowns
and Friendships

The high school football coach walked over to the shy young man standing by the edge of the playing field.

"What position are you interested in, son?" he asked.

"I'd like to be a linebacker," said Gale Sayers softly.

The coach shook his head. "That would be a waste of your talent. You'd be a better halfback. A halfback needs to run. And you run like the wind!"

A Super Player, A Shy Man

Gale Sayers could indeed run fast. He could also change direction with lightning speed. He would use his head and shoulders to **fake** movement in one direction. Then he would take off like a flash a different way.

fake
pretend

Gale Sayers became the star halfback of his high school team. More than 100 colleges flooded him with offers during his last year of high school. He

Sayers carrying the ball for the University of Kansas

chose to go to the University of Kansas. There he excited fans and teammates alike. He rushed for 2,675 yards. He became the biggest name in Kansas's football history. Off the field, however, Sayers remained the same quiet person he had always been.

In 1965, Gale Sayers was signed by the Chicago Bears. There Sayers met another halfback named Brian Piccolo. Piccolo was a small Italian kid from the Southeast. Sayers was a large African-American from the Midwest. Sayers was very quiet. Piccolo was always laughing and clowning around. No one expected the two men to become friends. After all, they were both trying to win the same job.

Yet Sayers and Piccolo did become good friends. Sayers learned to enjoy Piccolo's **relaxed** ways. And Piccolo learned to understand Sayers' shyness.

relaxed
easy-going

Sayers sprints for yardage.

Six Touchdowns!

By the middle of their first year, Sayers had won the spot of starting halfback. Piccolo became his back-up. As the season went on, Sayers became well-known for his end runs. He would get the ball then run wide, sweeping around the other team. He led the Bears to eight straight wins. By December, he had scored sixteen **touchdowns**. Heading into the last game, he hoped to score five more. That would set a new National Football League record for the season.

The last game was played at Chicago's Wrigley Field against the San Francisco Forty-Niners. Time after time, Sayers dashed forward with the ball. He scored one touchdown then another and another. In the third quarter, he scored for the fourth time that day.

Late in the game he was handed the ball again. Sayers charged down the middle of the field. He was **tackled** just as he was about to make a touchdown. As he threw himself into the end zone, the crowd went wild. Sayers had done it! He had scored five touchdowns in the game. And he had broken the season record with 21 touchdowns!

Once again Sayers got the ball. The Bears were 85 yards away from a touchdown. Sayers **streaked** past two men who were trying to tackle him. Farther down the field he **dodged** two others.

At last only one man stood between him and the end zone. As that player came at him, Sayers faked one way, then another. He slipped past the player and ran the ball into the end zone. With that, he tied the record for the most touchdowns in a single game. And he earned a name as one of the fastest halfbacks ever.

touchdowns
six-point scores made in football

tackled
brought to the ground

streaked
moved very fast

dodged
ran around something that was in the way

61

The Struggles of Two Great Men

Over the next two seasons, Sayers played beautifully. Then, during a game in his fourth season, he was hit hard in the knees. As the fans looked on in **horror**, he was carried off the field.

From then on, Sayers had knee problems. He had **operation** after operation. But he never again showed the blinding speed of his early days. As Sayers **struggled** to get his skills back, Brian Piccolo was there to help him. When Sayers lost hope, Piccolo would cheer him up by telling jokes.

By 1969, Sayers and Piccolo were playing side by side. Sayers was strong enough to play halfback again. And Piccolo had switched to fullback. As the season went on, however, Piccolo developed a bad cough. Every week it grew worse. Soon tests brought terrible news. Brian Piccolo had cancer.

Like everyone else, Gale Sayers was shocked. "Brian helped me fight back after my knee operations," he thought. "Now it's my turn to help him."

Sayers made himself shake off his shyness. Suddenly he was the one telling jokes, trying to make Piccolo smile. For the first time in his life, Sayers became a leader. He stood up in front of all the Chicago Bear players and asked them to win a game for Piccolo.

In May of 1970, Sayers won a Professional Football Writers award. The group named him "the most **courageous** player in football" for his struggle with his knees. Sayers was honored. But he told everyone that the award really belonged to Brian Piccolo.

horror
a feeling of great fear

operation
when a doctor cuts into a person's body in order to fix something

struggled
worked hard

courageous
very brave

Two weeks later, Brian Piccolo died. The following year, Gale Sayers quit playing football because of his knees. In the space of a few short months, football had lost two great heroes.

Brian Piccolo (1943–1970)

Vocabulary Skill Builder

■ Complete the following sentences by writing the missing word in each space. Choose from the words in the box. When you are finished, the letters in the boxes will tell you one thing that made Gale Sayers a star.

tackled	fake	courageous	relaxed	struggled
streaked	horror	operation	dodged	touchdowns

1. When players tried to tackle Sayers, they were often _____ .

   _ _ _ ☐ _ _

2. When Sayers was carried off the field, fans watched in _____ .

   _ _ ☐ _ _ _

3. Football players are often _____ .

   _ _ _ _ _ ☐ _

4. Sayers moved his head and shoulders as a _____ .

   _ ☐ _ _

5. After his knee operations, Sayers _____ .

   _ ☐ _ _ _ _ _ _ _

6. Gale Sayers ran so fast that people said he _____ .

   ☐ _ _ _ _ _ _ _

7. Gale Sayers had to have a knee _____ .

   _ ☐ _ _ _ _ _ _ _

8. Brian Piccolo's style was _____ .

   _ ☐ _ _ _ _ _ _

9. Sayers won an award for being _____ .

   _ _ _ _ _ _ ☐ _ _

10. In one game, Sayers scored six _____ .

    _ _ _ _ _ ☐ _ _ _

Read and Remember

■ Answer the questions.

1. Why did the high school coach say that Gale Sayers should be a halfback instead of a linebacker? _____

   _____

2. What was Gale Sayers like when he was not playing football?

   _____

3. What happened in the last game of Sayer's first season with the Chicago Bears? _____

   _____

4. What made Gale Sayers lose some of his speed? _____

   _____

5. Who did Gale Sayers think was the bravest player in football?

   _____

Write Your Ideas

■ Pretend you are Gale Sayers. You want to ask the Chicago Bears to win a game for Brian Piccolo. Write a short speech that you would give to your teammates about this.

_____

_____

_____

_____

_____

_____

_____

Joe Namath

Winning With Style

glamorous
exciting and unusual

"Come on, Joe," said Frank Namath to his son. "Let me show you around the mill." Frank Namath had come to the United States from Hungary. He was a steelworker in Beaver Falls, Pennsylvania.

"Well, what do you think?" asked Frank after he took Joe around.

"It's okay," said Joe politely. But he knew deep down that he never wanted to work in such a hot, noisy place. He dreamed of something much more **glamorous**.

Wild and Free

Joe was the youngest of four sports-loving brothers. When his brothers needed another player, they often used Joe—even though he was only five years old. Joe's mother, Rose, said, "When the boys needed a quarterback, Joe was it. They taught him to throw the ball over telephone wires. Because he was so small, they agreed not to tackle him."

The Namath boys were always playing sports or running wild through the neighborhood. They swam in the nearby river. They wandered through deserted buildings. They collected rocks down by the railroad tracks. It never bothered Namath that his family lived in a poor part of town. He didn't care that they had no money. "We had everything," he later said. "It was just great growing up there."

Namath scrambles to throw.

When Joe Namath entered high school in 1957, he was still a small, scrappy kid. In his second year at Beaver Falls High, he barely made the football team. He was the smallest player on the team. He played only two minutes all season. The next year he got the job of starting quarterback. He was so bad, however, that he was benched after only three games.

Namath taking snap from center

Namath didn't give up. That summer he worked hard to improve his skills. He later said, "If you want something bad enough, you'll get it if you work for it."

In his last year of high school, Namath was again named starting quarterback.

By this time he was a great **athlete**. He led the football team to the Western Pennsylvania championship. He also starred on the baseball and basketball teams.

By the time Namath finished high school, everybody wanted him. Fifty-two colleges offered him football scholarships. Six major league baseball teams hoped to sign him. The Chicago Cubs offered him $50,000 to sign with them. That was a huge sum of money in those days. But Namath's parents wanted Joe to go to college. So he went to the University of Alabama.

The Making of Broadway Joe

At first, Namath didn't like being 900 miles from home. But he was a fun-loving person. He soon made many friends. In fact, Namath spent too much time having fun. In his junior year, Namath stayed out past **curfew**. Coach Bear Bryant was **furious**. "That's it, Namath," Bryant said. "I'm **suspending** you from the team."

Namath was crushed. But it was an important lesson. If he wanted to play football under Bear Bryant, he had to play by the rules. In his last year, Namath came back to set many Alabama passing records **despite** an injury to his right knee. Bryant later said, "Joe Namath was the greatest athlete I ever coached."

In 1965, Namath entered professional football. At that time, there were two leagues: the National Football League (NFL) and the American Football League (AFL). The NFL had been around for many years, but the AFL was only five years old.

athlete
person who is trained in sports

curfew
a set time when a person has to come home

furious
very angry

suspending
not letting someone be part of something

despite
even though

merge
join together and
become one

competing
playing against

personality
what a person is like
to be around

Later, the AFL would **merge** with the NFL. In 1965, however, the two leagues were **competing** with each other for both fans and players. Teams from both leagues went after Joe Namath.

Namath signed with the AFL's New York Jets. The Jets came up with the most money ever offered a beginning player. The Jets wanted Namath because of his talent. They also wanted him because he had a colorful **personality**.

He was someone fans would notice. The Jets hoped Namath could win fans away from the New York Giants of the NFL.

Namath did gain the attention of fans. He went to many parties and spent lots of money. His wild ways earned him the nickname "Broadway Joe." Newspapers were filled with stories of him.

Broadway Joe and Super Bowl III

When it came to football, Namath's first problem was with his own teammates. A knee operation kept him off the field during many practices. Some players didn't like to see a highly-paid rookie skipping all the hard work. Namath didn't want to have enemies on his own team. So one day he spoke up at a meeting. He told his teammates, "All I'm asking is that you don't judge me for the money or what the newspapers say, that you let me get out on the field and play football."

Eventually, Namath's charm and skill on the field won over his teammates. He was a fine passer. He led his team to a second-place finish. Over the next couple of years, he became even better. And so did the Jets. In 1968, they won the AFL title. That gave them the right to play the NFL's Baltimore Colts in Super Bowl III.

Namath looking for a receiver downfield

No one expected the Jets to win. In the past two Super Bowls, the NFL team had crushed the AFL team. Everyone thought the same thing would happen again this year. Most people felt that the Colts would win by at least three touchdowns. Only one person really believed the Jets stood a chance. That person was Joe Namath. He announced, "We are going to win. I **guarantee** it!"

Namath kept his promise. The Jets stunned the Colts in Super Bowl III, beating them 16 to 7. Namath was named the game's Most Valuable Player. "Broadway Joe" had succeeded beyond his wildest dreams.

guarantee
promise

Vocabulary Skill Builder

■ Write a paragraph using these three words from the story.

guarantee: promise
despite: even though
furious: very angry

_____

_____

_____

_____

_____

_____

_____

_____

_____

_____

Part B

■ Match each word with its meaning.

____ 1. athlete

____ 2. personality

____ 3. curfew

____ 4. glamorous

____ 5. merge

____ 6. competing

____ 7. suspending

a. exciting and unusual

b. join together

c. person who is trained in sports

d. not letting a person be part of something

e. playing against

f. the time when a person has to come home

g. what a person is like to be around

Read and Remember

■ Answer the questions.

1. How did Joe Namath feel about his neighborhood? _____

_____

2. Why was Joe Namath suspended from the football team during his junior year in college? _____

_____

3. What nickname did Joe Namath earn? _____

_____

4. Why were some Jets players unhappy when Joe Namath first joined their team? _____

_____

5. Who believed the Jets would beat the Colts in the 1968 Super Bowl?

_____

Think and Apply—Finding the Sequence

■ Number the sentences to show the order in which things happened in the story. The first one is done for you.

_____ 1. Joe Namath signed with the AFL's New York Jets.

_____ 2. The New York Jets beat the Baltimore Colts in Super Bowl III.

_____ 3. Coach Bear Bryant suspended Joe Namath.

__1__ 4. Joe Namath's brothers taught him how to throw a football over telephone wires.

_____ 5. Joe Namath was offered scholarships by 52 colleges.

Earl Campbell

Power Runner

*S*ix miles outside of Tyler, Texas, stands the small tin-roofed hut where Earl Campbell grew up. Nearby is the big brick house Campbell built for his mother. He wanted to build it "so that when she lies down at night she can't see the Big Dipper." The hut stands as a reminder of how far football has taken Earl Campbell.

Determined to Change

Earl Campbell was born on March 29, 1955. He was the sixth of eleven children. His father died when Campbell was just 11 years old. That made life very hard for the family.

Campbell was unhappy. He didn't want to work in the rose fields on his family's farm. He wanted to be out having a good time. He started hanging out with a bad crowd. "I never really liked the country life when I was growing up," he later said. "I was always searching for something else."

Then one night, when he was 13, Campbell started to walk into town. It promised to be another night of getting into trouble. Suddenly, he changed his mind. He saw that his life was going nowhere. Earl Campbell decided to get **serious** about his future.

Football Star

Campbell set a new **goal** in life. He wanted to be a great running back. He worked hard to meet this goal. In his last year at John Tyler High School, he scored 28 touchdowns. Many colleges wanted him. He could have been **admitted** to any of them. But he chose the University of Texas.

serious
being thoughtful and having a sense of purpose

goal
something a person hopes to do or be

admitted
accepted into a class or school

Campbell played with the Oilers after winning the Heisman Trophy at the University of Texas.

Campbell became an **incredible** college player. In 1974, his first year, he ran for 928 yards. The next year he did even better. In 1976, he was injured. But in his last year, Campbell really took off. He rushed for 1,744 yards and scored 114 points. He won the Heisman Trophy as the best college player in the country. Barry Switzer, coach for the University of Oklahoma, praised Campbell's talent. He said, "Earl Campbell is the greatest football player I've ever seen."

Taking the NFL by Storm

Most **experts** agreed. They **rated** Campbell as a future NFL star. The Houston Oilers made him the top pick in the entire **draft**. They hoped he would **immediately** become a star. Campbell did not disappoint them. Things began to **click** right away for Campbell and the Oilers. He was so good he was named Rookie of the Year *and* MVP!

His best game came against the Miami Dolphins. By the fourth quarter, he had scored three times. He was worn out. But he managed to rush for 81 yards and yet another touchdown! Said the Oilers head coach O. A. ("Bum") Phillips, "You've got to give him the ball twenty, twenty-five times a game..."

Campbell played six years for the Oilers and two years for the New Orleans Saints. His speed made him a great running back. He won the MVP award in each of his first three years. He stopped playing football in 1986. **Altogether**, he gained over 9,400 yards. That makes Earl Campbell one of the best pro runners in history.

Earl Campbell ended his career playing for the New Orleans Saints

Today, Earl Campbell enjoys working with children. In his free time, he started the Earl Campbell Crusade for Kids. He also hopes to turn his ranch home into a camp for young people.

Vocabulary Skill Builder

■ Use the clues to complete the puzzle. Choose from the words in the box.

serious
goal
admitted
incredible
experts
rated
draft
immediately
click
altogether

Across

1. right away
3. fall into place
5. something you work toward
7. accepted into
8. people who know a lot about something

Down

1. amazing
2. completely
4. not fooling around
6. time when teams pick new players
9. put in order

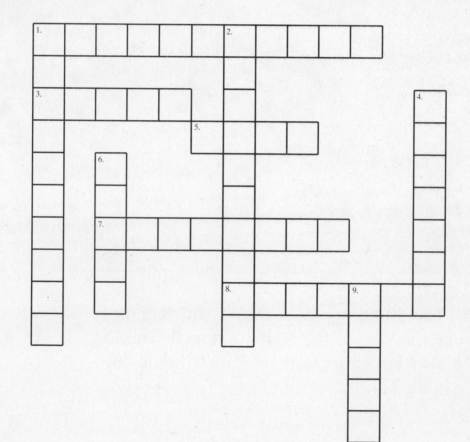

Read and Remember

■ Find the best ending for each sentence. Fill in the circle next to it.

1. When he was young, Campbell lived in
   ○ a. a tin-roofed hut.   ○ b. a large brick house.   ○ c. an apartment.

2. Earl Campbell grew up in a
   ○ a. small family.   ○ b. foster family.   ○ c. large family.

3. Campbell wanted to be a
   ○ a. running back.   ○ b. quarterback.   ○ c. wide receiver.

4. Campbell won the Heisman Trophy when he was a
   ○ a. junior.   ○ b. sophomore.   ○ c. senior.

5. Campbell's first year with the Houston Oilers was
   ○ a. a great success.   ○ b. a big disappointment.
   ○ c. not great but not bad.

Write Your Ideas

■ Write three important facts you learned about Earl Campbell.

1. _____
   _____
   _____

2. _____
   _____
   _____

3. _____
   _____
   _____

Terry Bradshaw

A Question of Confidence

chant
shouting the same
words over and over

exhibition
just for show—not
part of the real
season

appearance
doing something in
front of a group of
people

terrified
very scared

churn
to stir or move with
force

huddle
group of players
standing close
together

"We want Bradshaw! We want Bradshaw!" The **chant** rolled across the football field. The crowd had come to watch the Pittsburgh Steelers play an **exhibition** game. But what people really wanted was to see Terry Bradshaw, the Steelers' new quarterback.

Bradshaw finally got his chance to play. It was his big moment—his first **appearance** in pro football. Suddenly he was **terrified**. What if he made mistakes? What if he failed? As he walked on the field, he felt his stomach **churn**. Standing in his first team **huddle**, Terry Bradshaw got sick.

Too Much Pressure

Bradshaw calmed down enough to help the Steelers win the game. He also played well in four other exhibition games. But when the 1970 season began, he **floundered**. Bradshaw was a 22-year-old country boy. He had a strong arm and a real love of football. He had been a star quarterback at Louisiana Tech. But he was not ready for the pressure of playing pro football.

When Bradshaw came to Pittsburgh, the Steelers were a losing team. Coach Chuck Noll was hoping Bradshaw could turn the team around. Steelers fans were all hoping the same thing. This was a huge **burden** for Bradshaw to bear. He felt very nervous.

floundered
had trouble doing something

burden
load

Bradshaw goes back to pass.

This led him to play badly. Soon players and fans alike were saying unkind things about him. "What a dumb guy!" they said. "He's not smart enough to lead a pro team."

Bradshaw later described the 1970 season this way: "I wanted so badly to make the Steelers a winner. Maybe I wanted it too much, put too much pressure on myself. I made mistakes—plenty of mistakes. I was so **embarrassed** . . . The way I felt, I didn't know if I wanted to play football anymore."

embarrassed
felt foolish

You're Going to Make Us Winners

Over the next three years, the team began winning games, and Bradshaw began playing better. But he hurt his shoulder in 1973. At the start of the 1974 season, he was told he would no longer be starting quarterback. He would be a back-up for quarterback Joe Gilliam. Bradshaw felt he had hit rock bottom.

Coach Noll, however, still felt that Terry Bradshaw had talent. In the middle of the 1974 season, he came to Bradshaw.

"I think you're a better quarterback than Gilliam," Noll said. "So here's what I've decided. From now on, you're the starting quarterback, no matter what. Go out and make your mistakes. Don't worry about it. You're going to make us winners."

A Different Player

From that moment on, Terry Bradshaw was a different player. Knowing that the coach believed in him made Bradshaw feel better. He thought, "If the coach has that much confidence in me, maybe I really can make us winners." With this new

Bradshaw talks to a coach.

attitude, Bradshaw led his team to victory after victory. At the end of the 1974 season, the Steelers rolled to their first Super Bowl win.

attitude
a way of thinking or feeling

Over the next five years, the Steelers won three more Super Bowls. Terry Bradshaw became the first quarterback to lead his team to four NFL championships. In doing so, he proved that he was certainly not "dumb." By the time he retired in 1984, he had played on two All-Pro teams, in three Pro Bowls, and had been named the most valuable player in two Super Bowls.

Vocabulary Skill Builder

■ Complete the following sentences by writing the missing word in each space. Choose from the words in the box. When you are finished, the letters in the boxes will tell you what Terry Bradshaw needed to become a great player.

exhibition	terrified	chant	appearance	attitude
embarrassed	huddle	burden	floundered	churn

1. Bradshaw got nervous when he heard the fans _____ .

2. Bradshaw's first Steelers game was an _____ .

3. In the 1970 season, Bradshaw _____ .

4. In his first Steelers game, Bradshaw was _____ .

5. Coach Noll helped Bradshaw develop a new _____ .

6. Bradshaw got sick in his first team _____ .

7. After his first season, Bradshaw felt _____ .

8. For Bradshaw, the pressure of being a quarterback for a pro team was a heavy _____ .

9. In his first game, Bradshaw felt his stomach _____ .

10. Fans waited for Bradshaw's _____ .

Read and Remember

■ Some of the statements below are true. Others are false. Place a check in front of the three things that Terry Bradshaw did.

_____ 1. Terry Bradshaw grew up in a big city.

_____ 2. Terry Bradshaw got sick during his first exhibition game with the Pittsburgh Steelers.

_____ 3. Terry Bradshaw quit football after one season with the Pittsburgh Steelers.

_____ 4. Terry Bradshaw became coach of the Steelers.

_____ 5. Terry Bradshaw led the Pittsburgh Steelers to their first Super Bowl win ever.

_____ 6. Terry Bradshaw proved that he was not "dumb."

Think and Apply—Main Ideas

■ Underline the two most important ideas from the story.

1. Terry Bradshaw became a great quarterback after he learned to believe in himself.

2. Terry Bradshaw hurt his shoulder in 1973.

3. Terry Bradshaw went to Louisiana Tech before joining the Pittsburgh Steelers.

4. When Terry Bradshaw first joined the Pittsburgh Steelers, he was too nervous to show how well he could really play.

5. Terry Bradshaw was the Pittsburgh Steelers' back-up quarterback at the start of the 1974 season.

Glossary

ability, page 48
Ability means being able to do something well. She has a great deal of musical ability.

adjusted, page 48
If a person adjusted to something, it means he or she got used to it. At first Jesse was homesick, but then he adjusted to summer camp and had fun.

admitted, page 75
To be admitted to a school is to be accepted into it as a student.

advice, page 18
Advice is a set of ideas offered to help someone solve a problem.

aid, page 25
To bring aid is to bring help. Aid in the form of food, medicine, and other supplies was taken to the flooded city.

altogether, page 76
Altogether means completely.

ankles, page 24
The ankles are the parts of the body that connect feet to legs.

announcer, page 35
An announcer is a person who describes a game to people who are watching it on TV or listening to it on the radio.

appearance, page 80
If you make an appearance, you show up or perform in front of a group of people. The appearance of the famous singer caused much excitement.

architecture, page 17
Architecture is the art of designing buildings.

assists, page 43
Assists are times when a player passes the ball to a teammate who then scores a basket.

athlete, page 69
An athlete is a person who is trained in sports.

attitude, page 83
An attitude is a way of thinking or feeling. He had a bad attitude about doing homework.

average, page 5
A batting average is the number of hits a player has for every thousand times at bat.

barrier, page 11
A barrier is something that keeps people from joining together. If two people do not speak the same language, they face a language barrier.

brilliantly, page 18
To do something brilliantly means to do it very well.

bum, page 18
A bum is a person who performs poorly.

burden, page 81
A burden is something that is very heavy or hard to handle. Taking care of her little sister was a great burden to Lisa.

career, page 5
A career is the work that a person does over the course of his or her life.

celebration, page 47
A celebration is a special party held in honor of a certain person or event.

ceremony, page 6
A ceremony is a special act that is part of some important event. When people get married, they have a wedding ceremony.

championship, page 32
A championship is a contest held to see which team is best.

chant, page 80
A chant is the shouting or singing of the same words over and over.

churn, page 80
To churn is to stir or move in a forceful way. The rushing water churned around the rocks.

civil rights, page 34
Civil rights means giving all people the same rights. Before civil rights laws were passed, African-Americans did not have the same rights as white people.

click, page 76
When things click, troubles disappear and everything falls into place.

clumsy, page 30
To be clumsy is to move your body in an awkward way. The baby was just learning to walk and was very clumsy.

clutch, page 48
A clutch shot is a shot that is made at a very important point in the game.

competing, page 70
Someone who is competing is playing against others in an effort to win something. The two teams were competing for the trophy.

confidence, page 54
Confidence is the belief you have in yourself and your skills.

confused, page 22
To be confused is to be mixed up or not sure about something.

constant, page 55
Constant means all the time.

contract, page 10
A contract is an agreement to do a certain job for a certain amount of pay.

courageous, page 62
A courageous person is a person who is very brave.

created, page 23
If you created something, you made something or caused something to happen. The circus created great excitement when it came to town.

cripple, page 18
To cripple means to cause lasting harm.

curfew, page 69
A curfew is a set time in the evening when a person has to come home. Tom's parents set an eleven o'clock curfew for the weekend.

dazzled, page 40
To be dazzled is to be amazed.

defensive, page 31
A defensive player is one who tries to keep the other team from scoring.

despite, page 69
Despite means doing something even though there are reasons why it is hard to do.

determined, page 46
To be determined is to have a strong wish or need to do something. She was determined to win the race.

disease, page 6
A disease is a sickness.

dismal, page 53
Dismal means terrible.

dodged, page 61
If you dodged something, it means you ran around something that was in the way.

draft, page 76
The draft is when teams choose which new players they want. The best college players are drafted by professional teams.

dribbling, page 40
Dribbling a basketball means bouncing a basketball as you move down the court.

eager, page 52
To be eager is to want something very much and to be in a hurry to get it.

elected, page 19
Someone who is elected is someone who has been chosen by a vote.

embarrassed, page 82
To be embarrassed is to feel foolish or ashamed. I was embarrassed when I didn't know the answer to the teacher's question.

exhibition, page 80
An exhibition game is a game that is played just for show. It does not count as part of the real season.

experts, page 76
Experts are people who know a lot about a certain thing.

extremely, page 23
Extremely means very. To be extremely happy is to be very happy.

fake, page 58
To fake is to pretend something is real in order to fool someone. He faked being sick, so he wouldn't have to take the test.

fielding, page 5
Fielding means going after a baseball that has been hit and either catching it or picking it up.

final, page 48
Final means last. The final game is the last game.

floundered, page 81
If a person floundered, he or she had trouble doing something and did it poorly.

furious, page 69
To be furious is to be very angry.

future, page 18
The future is the time yet to come.

glamorous, page 66
If something is glamorous is seems exciting and unusual to others. She thought it would be glamorous to be a movie star.

glories, page 26
Glories are people or things that bring feelings of honor and pride. Mount Rushmore is one of the glories of America.

goal, page 75
A goal is something a person hopes to do or be.

guarantee, page 71
A guarantee is a promise to do something.

guiding, page 55
A person who is guiding you is teaching or directing you.

heartbroken, page 26
To be heartbroken is to be filled with sadness.

hobbling, page 47
A person who is hobbling is having trouble walking. After I fell, I got up and hobbled to the park bench.

horror, page 62
Horror is a feeling of great fear.

huddle, page 80
In football, the players of one team stand close together and form a huddle. They make plans for the next play while they are in the huddle.

immediately, page 76
To do something immediately is to do it right away.

immigrant, page 12
An immigrant is a person who moves to a different country from where he or she was born and raised. Many immigrants from Latin America live in the United States.

impressed, page 43
To be impressed is to feel that someone has done something important or special. I was impressed by the children's artwork.

incredible, page 76
Something that is incredible is so amazing that it is hard to believe.

injuries, page 4
Injuries are damage that has been done to the body. Cuts, bruises, and broken bones are examples of injuries.

insults, page 43
Insults are remarks that are made that hurt people's feelings. The angry boy shouted insults at his sister.

involved, page 13
To be involved with something is to be connected or linked with it.

lizard, page 55
A lizard is a small, quick animal that looks like a tiny alligator. It has four legs, a long tail, and rough skin.

merge, page 70
To merge is to join two or more things together and make them one.

monument, page 7
A monument is an object built to remember someone.

Most Valuable Player, page 12
Most Valuable Player is the name given to the player who helps the team the most over the course of the season. The Most Valuable Player is chosen by a vote of sports writers.

offense, page 43
To play offense is to attack the other team and try to score points. Offense is the opposite of defense.

operation, page 62
An operation is when a doctor cuts open part of a person's body in order to fix something.

opponents, page 55
Opponents are the players on the other team.

overtime, page 49
Overtime is time added to the regular playing time of a game to break a tie score.

paralyzed, page 13
To be paralyzed is to lose all movement and feeling in a certain part of your body.

pennants, page 12
Pennants are the flags given to baseball teams who finish first in their league.

percent, page 40
Percent means how many parts out of each one hundred parts. Five percent means five out of each one hundred parts.

personality, page 70
Personality means what a person is like to be around. Different people have different personalities. Some people are shy, some are friendly, etc.

pressure, page 55
Pressure is a strong force put on someone to do something.

professional, page 34
A professional is someone who is paid to do a job. The best basketball players in college often join professional teams.

quarterback, page 52
A quarterback is the leader of a football team. The quarterback usually calls the plays for the team and is the one who passes the ball.

rated, page 76
If you rated something, you compared it to other things and put it in a certain order.

rebounded, page 32
If you rebounded, it means you got the basketball after someone missed a shot.

relaxed, page 60
A relaxed person is someone who is easy-going and not worried.

retired, page 6
When a number is retired, it is set aside so that no other player can use it. A team retires a number as a way of honoring a great player.

rival, page 18
A rival is a member of another team. The two friends became rivals when they joined different baseball teams.

rookie, page 12
A rookie is a person who is playing his or her first year of professional sports.

scheme, page 23
A scheme is a plan to do something.

scholarships, page 41
Scholarships are gifts of money offered to a student to help him or her pay for school.

serious, page 75
To be serious is to be thoughtful and have a sense of purpose instead of being silly and fooling around.

soared, page 12
If something soared, it went very high.

sponsoring, page 16
To sponsor an event is to plan it and take responsibility for it.

stadium, page 6
A stadium is a place where sports such as baseball or football are played. In a stadium, rows of seats are built around an open field.

streaked, page 61
Streaked means moved very fast. Lightning streaked across the night sky.

struggled, page 62
If you struggled, it means you worked very hard at something.

stunned, page 10
To be stunned is to be amazed.

success, page 18
A success is a person who does something well.

suspending, page 69
Suspending a player means not letting him or her be part of the team for a certain length of time. Suspending a person is a way of punishing him or her.

swished, page 48
If something swished, it made a soft, brushing sound. The basketball swished through the net.

tackled, page 61
To be tackled is to be brought to the ground by another person.

talents, page 40
Talents are skills that people have. If you have many talents, there are many things that you do well.

terrific, page 23
If something is terrific, it is wonderful.

terrified, page 80
To be terrified is to be very scared.

threat, page 55
A threat is a danger.

touchdowns, page 61
A touchdown is the scoring of six points in a football game. A touchdown is made when a player carries the ball into the end zone or catches it while standing in the end zone.

tournament, page 48
A tournament is a contest made up of several games.

tragic, page 6
Something that is tragic is very sad.

treatment, page 34
Treatment is the way people act toward someone or something.

undefeated, page 40
To be undefeated is to have no losses.

unfortunately, page 23
Unfortunately means causing bad luck. Unfortunately, he got sick and could not run in the race.

vast, page 34
Something that is vast is very large.

victories, page 32
Victories are games that are won.

Keeping Score

1. Count the number of correct answers you have for each activity.
2. Write these numbers in the boxes in the chart.
3. Ask your teacher to give you a score (maximum score 5) for Write Your Ideas.
4. Add up the numbers to get a final score.

Stories	Vocabulary Skill Builder	Read and Remember	Think and Apply	Write Your Ideas	Score
Lou Gehrig					/20
Roy Campanella					/17
Sandy Koufax					/20
Roberto Clemente					/18
Bill Russell					/20
Oscar Robertson					/25
Jerry West					/20
Walt Frazier					/15
Gale Sayers					/20
Joe Namath					/20
Earl Campbell					/18
Terry Bradshaw					/15

Answer Key

Lou Gehrig   Pages 2-9

Vocabulary Skill Builder

Across: 2. tragic, 4. average,
7. retired, 9. injuries, 10. monument

Down: 1. fielding, 3. career,
5. ceremony, 6. stadium, 8. disease

Read and Remember

1. Gehrig played in 2,130 games in a row in spite of injuries.
2. His batting average dropped below .300.
3. They told him he had a rare disease that would soon kill him.
4. He hugged Lou Gehrig.
5. They held Lou Gehrig Day, retired his number, and built a monument.

Write Your Ideas

Answers will vary.

Roy Campanella   Pages 10-15

Vocabulary Skill Builder

Part A: 1. contract, 2. barrier,
            3. Most Valuable Player,
            4. pennants, 5. paralyzed

Part B: 1-d, 2-b, 3-e, 4-a, 5-c

Read and Remember 2, 3, 4

Think and Apply—Cause and Effect

1. at that time African-Americans couldn't play in the major leagues.
2. they didn't like the idea of African-Americans in the major leagues.
3. he hoped the warm weather would help him play even better.
4. a car accident left him paralyzed.

Sandy Koufax   Pages 16-21

Vocabulary Skill Builder

Part A: Answers will vary.

Part B: 1-a, 2-c, 3-c, 4-a, 5-b, 6-b,
            7-a

Read and Remember

1-b, 2-c, 3-c, 4-a, 5-b

Write Your Ideas

Answers will vary.

Roberto Clemente   Pages 22-29

Vocabulary Skill Builder

Part A: 1-d, 2-e, 3-c, 4-f, 5-b, 6-a

Part B: 1-b, 2-c, 3-b, 4-a

Read and Remember 1, 4, 6

Think and Apply—Drawing Conclusions

1. he didn't know the language or the customs.
2. they believed he was a great player.
3. he wanted to do something for his country.
4. he wanted to make sure the supplies got to the people who needed them.
5. a new plane could not be found on such short notice.

Bill Russell   Pages 30-37

Vocabulary Skill Builder

1. treatment, 2. championship,
3. defensive, 4. civil rights,
5. rebounded, 6. clumsy,
7. victories, 8. professional,
9. announcer, 10. vast

CODE WORDS—THE CELTICS

Read and Remember

1-b, 2-c, 3-a, 4-c, 5-c

Write Your Ideas

Answers will vary.

Oscar Robertson   Pages 38-45

Vocabulary Skill Builder

Part A: 1-b, 2-g, 3-e, 4-a, 5-f, 6-c,
            7-d

Part B: Answers will vary.

Read and Remember

1. His mother brought it home from

the family she cooked for.

2. She wanted him to have more time to practice basketball.

3. They didn't like him because he was an African-American.

4. The team did not have enough other good players.

5. No one else has done so many things so well.

Think and Apply—Fact or Opinion?
1-O, 2-F, 3-F, 4-O, 5-O, 6-O, 7-F, 8-F, 9-O, 10-O

Jerry West   Pages 46-51

Vocabulary Skill Builder
Across: 3. hobbling, 6. determined, 7. tournament, 9. overtime, 10. clutch
Down: 1. swished, 2. ability, 4. adjusted, 5. celebration, 8. final

Read and Remember
1-b, 2-b, 3-c, 4-a, 5-b

Write Your Ideas
Answers will vary.

Walt Frazier   Pages 52-57

Vocabulary Skill Builder
  Part A: 1. quarterback, 2. eager, 3. dismal, 4. confidence, 5. guiding
  Part B: 1-b, 2-a, 3-c, 4-b, 5-b
Read and Remember 1, 4, 6
Think and Apply—Main Idea 1, 5

Gale Sayers   Pages 58-65

Vocabulary Skill Builder
1. dodged, 2. horror, 3. tackled, 4. fake, 5. struggled, 6. streaked, 7. operation, 8. relaxed, 9. courageous, 10. touchdowns
CODE WORDS—GREAT SPEED

Read and Remember
1. Halfbacks need to be fast, and Sayers was very fast.

2. He was quiet and shy.

3. Sayers tied the record for the most touchdowns in a single game.

4. He hurt his knee.

5. He thought Brian Piccolo was the bravest player.

Write Your Ideas Answers will vary.

Joe Namath   Pages 66-73

Vocabulary Skill Builder
  Part A: Answers will vary.
  Part B: 1-c, 2-g, 3-f, 4-a, 5-b, 6-e, 7-d
Read and Remember
1. He loved it and thought it was a great place to grow up.

2. He stayed out past his curfew.

3. He earned the nickname "Broadway Joe."

4. Namath was being paid lots of money and skipping practices.

5. Joe Namath believed the Jets would win.

Think and Apply—Finding the Sequence 4, 5, 3, 1, 2

Earl Campbell   Pages 74-79

Vocabulary Skill Builder
Across: 1. immediately, 3. click, 5. goal, 7. admitted, 8. experts
Down: 1. incredible, 2. altogether, 4. serious, 6. draft, 9. rated

Read and Remember
1-a, 2-c, 3-a, 4-c, 5-a

Write Your Ideas
Answers will vary.

Terry Bradshaw   Pages 80-85

Vocabulary Skill Builder
1. chant, 2. exhibition, 3. floundered, 4. terrified, 5. attitude, 6. huddle, 7. embarrassed, 8. burden, 9. churn, 10. appearance
CODE WORD—CONFIDENCE

Read and Remember 2, 5, 6
Think and Apply—Main Ideas 1, 4